THE
Influence
ᴼᶠ
RIGHTEOUS
WOMEN

THE
Influence
OF
RIGHTEOUS
WOMEN

DIETER F. UCHTDORF

DESERET
BOOK

SALT LAKE CITY, UTAH

Book design © Deseret Book Company
Art direction: Richard Erickson
Design: Sheryl Dickert Smith
Cover illustration © pluie_r/shutterstock.com
Interior illustration © miumi/shutterstock.com

Visit us at DeseretBook.com

ISBN 978-1-62972-337-2

Printed in the United States of America
Artistic Printing, Salt Lake City, UT

10   9   8   7   6   5   4   3   2   1

*T*he scriptures give us names of several women who have blessed individuals and generations with their spiritual gifts. Eve, the mother of all living; Sarah; Rebekah; Rachel; Martha; Elisabeth; and Mary, the mother of our Savior, will always be honored and remembered. The scriptures also mention women whose names are unknown to us but who bless our lives through their examples and teachings, like the woman of Samaria whom Jesus met at the well of Sychar (see John 4), the ideal wife and mother described in Proverbs 31, and the faithful woman who was made whole just by touching the Savior's clothes (see Mark 5:25–34).

As we look at the history of this earth and at the history of the restored Church of Jesus Christ, it becomes obvious that women hold a special place in our

Father's plan for the eternal happiness and well-being of His children.

I hope that my dear sisters throughout the world—grandmothers, mothers, aunts, and friends—never underestimate the power of their influence for good, especially in the lives of our precious children and youth!

President Heber J. Grant said, "Without the devotion and absolute testimony of the living God in the hearts of our mothers this Church would die."[1] And the writer of Proverbs said, "Train up a child in the way he should go: and when he is old, he will not depart from it" (Proverbs 22:6).

President Gordon B. Hinckley counseled the women of the Church:

"It is so tremendously important that the women of the Church stand strong and immovable for that which is correct and proper under the plan of the Lord. . . .

"We call upon the women of the Church to stand together for righteousness. They must begin in their own homes. They can teach it in their classes. They can voice it in their communities."[2]

There is a saying that big gates move on small hinges. Sisters, your example in seemingly small things will make

WITHOUT THE DEVOTION

and absolute testimony

—— OF ——

THE LIVING GOD

IN THE HEARTS OF

our mothers

this Church would die.

>>>>> HEBER J. GRANT <<<<<

a big difference in the lives of our young people. The way you dress and groom yourselves, the way you talk, the way you pray, the way you testify, the way you live every day will make the difference. This includes which TV shows you watch, which music you prefer, and how you use the Internet. If you love to go to the temple, the young people who value your example will also love to go. If you adapt your wardrobe to the temple garment and not the other way around, they will know what you consider important, and they will learn from you.

You are marvelous sisters and great examples. Our youth are blessed by you, and the Lord loves you for that.

AN EXAMPLE OF FAITH

Let me share some thoughts about Sister Carmen Reich, my mother-in-law, who was truly an elect lady. She embraced the gospel in a most difficult and dark time of her life, and she liberated herself from grief and sorrow.

As a young woman—a widow and the mother of two young girls—she freed herself from a world of old traditions and moved into a world of great spirituality. She embraced the teachings of the gospel, with its intellectual and spiritual power, on a fast track. When the missionaries gave her the Book of Mormon and invited her to read the verses they had marked, she read the whole book within only a few days. She learned things beyond the understanding of her peers because she learned them by the Spirit of God. She was the humblest of the humble, the wisest of the wise, because she was willing and pure enough to believe when God had spoken.

She was baptized on November 7, 1954. Only a few weeks after her baptism, she was asked by the missionary who baptized her to write her testimony. The missionary wanted to use her testimony in his teaching to help others feel the true spirit of conversion. Fortunately, the missionary kept the handwritten original for more than 40 years, and then he returned it to her as a very special and loving gift.

A TESTIMONY BORN OF THE SPIRIT

Let me share with you parts of her written testimony. Please keep in mind that she wrote these words only a few weeks after hearing about the gospel. Before the missionaries came, she had never heard anything about the Book of Mormon, Joseph Smith, or Mormons in general. In 1954 there were no temples outside the continental United States, except in Canada and Hawaii.

This is the English translation of Sister Reich's handwritten testimony:

"Special characteristics of The Church of Jesus Christ of Latter-day Saints that are not present in other religious communities include, above all, modern revelation given through the Prophet Joseph Smith.

"The Book of Mormon in its clear and pure language is next, with all the instructions and promises for the Church of Jesus Christ; it is truly a second witness, together with the Bible, that Jesus Christ lives.

"Bound together by faith in a personal God, that is, God the Father, God the Son, and the Holy Ghost, who facilitates prayer and also influences personally.

"Also, faith in the premortal life, the preexistence, the purpose of our earthly life, and our life after death is so valuable for us and especially interesting and informative. It is clearly laid out, and our lives receive new meaning and direction.

"The Church has given us the Word of Wisdom as a guide to keep body and spirit in the most perfect shape possible to realize our desire and goal. So we keep our bodies healthy and improve them. All this from the knowledge that we will take them up again after death in the same form.

"Totally new to me, of course, is temple work with its many sacred ordinances, having families together forever. All this was given through revelation to the Prophet Joseph Smith."

Carmen Reich, my dear mother-in-law, passed away in 2000 at age 83.

A UNIQUE FEMININE IDENTITY

The lives of women in the Church are a powerful witness that spiritual gifts, promises, and blessings of the Lord are given to all those who qualify, "that all may be benefited" (D&C 46:9; see vv. 9–26). The doctrines of the restored gospel create a wonderful and "unique feminine identity that encourages women to develop their abilities"[3] as true and literal daughters of God. Through serving in the Relief Society, Young Women, and Primary organizations—not to mention their private acts of love and service—women have always played and will always play an important part in helping "bring forth and establish the cause of Zion" (D&C 6:6). They

WHAT YOU SISTERS DO

TODAY

WILL DETERMINE HOW

THE PRINCIPLES OF THE RESTORED
GOSPEL CAN INFLUENCE THE
NATIONS OF THE WORLD

tomorrow.

IT WILL DETERMINE HOW

THESE HEAVENLY RAYS OF THE
GOSPEL WILL LIGHT EVERY LAND

in the future.

care for the poor and the sick; serve proselytizing, welfare, humanitarian, and other missions; teach children, youth, and adults; and contribute to the temporal and spiritual welfare of the Saints in many other ways.

Because their potential for good is so great and their gifts so diverse, women may find themselves in roles that vary with their circumstances in life. Some women, in fact, must fill many roles simultaneously. For this reason, Latter-day Saint women are encouraged to acquire an education and training that will qualify them both for homemaking and raising a righteous family and for earning a living outside the home if the occasion requires.

We are living in a great season for all women in the Church. Sisters, you are an essential part of our Heavenly Father's plan for eternal happiness; you are endowed with a divine birthright. You are the real builders of nations wherever you live, because strong homes of love and peace will bring security to any nation. I hope you understand that, and I hope the men of the Church understand it too.

What you sisters do today will determine how the principles of the restored gospel can influence the nations of the world tomorrow. It will determine how these heavenly rays of the gospel will light every land in the future.[4]

Though we often speak of the influence of women on future generations, please do not underestimate the influence you can have today. President David O. McKay said that the principal reason the Church was organized is "to make life sweet today, to give contentment to the heart today, to bring salvation today. . . .

"Some of us look forward to a time in the future—salvation and exaltation in the world to come—but today is part of eternity."[5]

BLESSINGS BEYOND IMAGINING

As you live up to this mission, in whatever life circumstance you find yourself—as a wife, as a mother, as a single mother, as a divorced woman, as a widowed or a single woman—the Lord our God will open up responsibilities and blessings far beyond your ability to imagine.

May I invite you to rise to the great potential within you. But don't reach beyond your capacity. Don't set goals beyond your capacity to achieve. Don't feel guilty or dwell on thoughts of failure. Don't compare yourself with others. Do the best you can, and the Lord will provide the rest. Have faith and confidence in Him, and you will see miracles happen in your life and the lives of your loved ones. The virtue of your own life will be a light to those who sit in darkness, because you are a living witness of the fulness of the gospel (see D&C 45:28). Wherever you have been planted on this beautiful but often troubled earth of ours, you can be the one to "succor the weak, lift up the hands which hang down, and strengthen the feeble knees" (D&C 81:5).

My dear sisters, as you live your daily life with all its blessings and challenges, let me assure you that the Lord loves you. He knows you. He listens to your prayers, and He answers those prayers, wherever on this world you may be. He wants you to succeed in this life and in eternity.

Brethren, I pray that we as priesthood holders—as husbands, fathers, sons, brothers, and friends of these choice women—may see them as the Lord sees them, as daughters of God with limitless potential to influence the world for good.

In the early days of the Restoration, the Lord spoke to Emma Smith through her husband, the Prophet Joseph Smith, giving her instructions and blessings:

"[Be] faithful and walk in the paths of virtue before me.
. . . Thou needest not fear. . . . Thou shalt lay aside the
things of this world, and seek for the things of a better.
. . . Lift up thy heart and rejoice. . . . And a crown of
righteousness thou shalt receive" (D&C 25:2, 9, 10, 13, 15).

Of this revelation, the Lord declared, "This is my
voice unto all" (verse 16).

Later, the Prophet Joseph Smith told the sisters, "If
you live up to your privileges, the angels cannot be re-
strained from being your associates."[6]

Of these truths I testify, and I extend to you my
love and my blessing as an Apostle of our Savior, the
Lord Jesus Christ.

NOTES

1. Heber J. Grant, *Gospel Standards*, comp. G. Homer Durham (1941), 151.
2. Gordon B. Hinckley, "Standing Strong and Immovable," *Worldwide Leadership Training Meeting* (2004), 20.
3. "Women, Roles of: Historical and Sociological Development," in Daniel H. Ludlow, ed., *Encyclopedia of Mormonism*, 5 vols. (1992), 4:1574.
4. See "Hark, All Ye Nations!" *Hymns of The Church of Jesus Christ of Latter-day Saints* (1985), no. 264.
5. David O. McKay, *Pathways to Happiness*, comp. Llewelyn R. McKay (1957), 291–92.
6. "Nauvoo Relief Society Minute Book," p. [38], The Joseph Smith Papers.